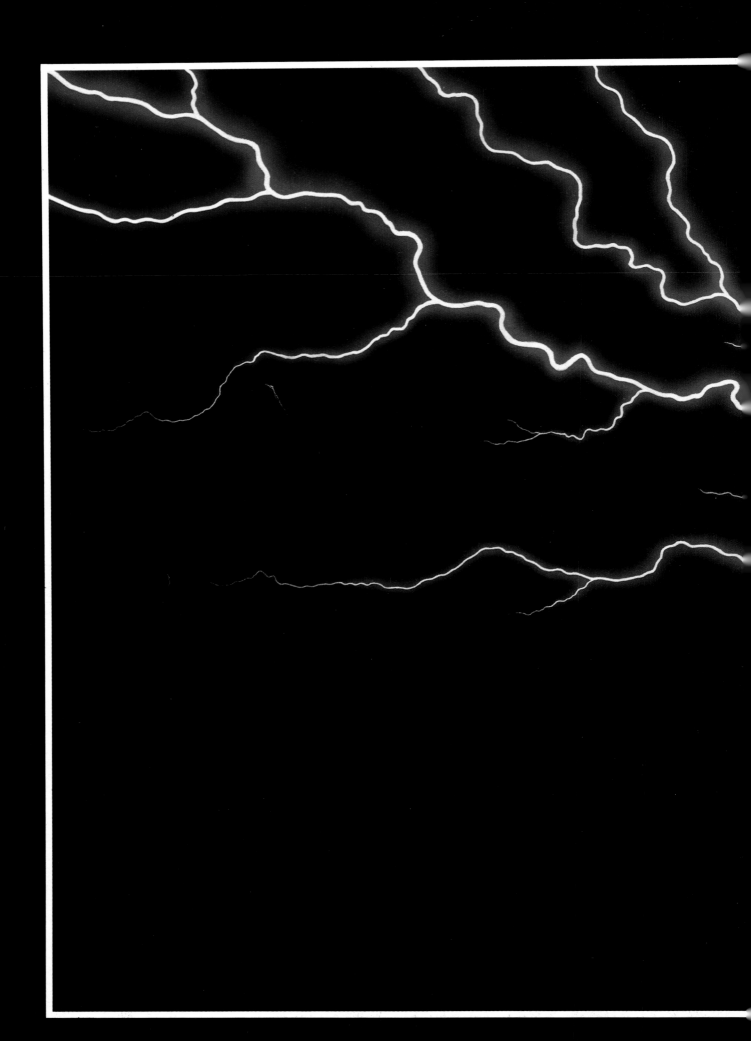

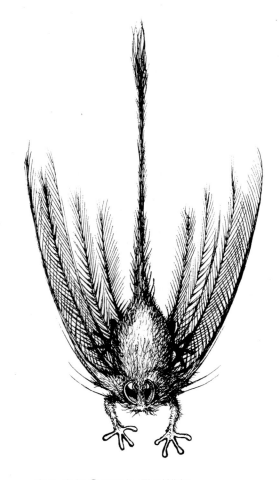

Design: Ian Hughes

A DRAGON'S WORLD IMPRINT
Dragon's World Ltd
Limpsfield, Surrey RH8 0DY
Great Britain

Hardback: ISBN 1 85028 058 4
Limpback: ISBN 1 85028 057 6

Reprinted 1988

Printed in Singapore

The Science Fiction and Fantasy World of TIM WHITE

FOREWORD

The future remains hidden from us and our past has become obscured by the passage of time – concealed in myths and legends. Imagination is our vehicle of exploration into the possibilities and Fantasy and Science Fiction is a realm where these transient thoughts pass into tangibility. The scope of these works is immense – spanning the past, present and future, from the credible to the incredible.

In an era which has witnessed extraordinary advances in technology, the boundaries between the plausible and the improbable are constantly shifting. Before this swiftly changing backdrop to the genre much fictional speculation has passed into fact. Perhaps the best known example is by Arthur C. Clarke, who proposed the use of orbital satellites for world-wide television in 1945.

Fantasy art has always provided a popular means of expression and for the contemporary artist the rapid growth of the Science Fiction and Fantasy scene is an ever-widening frame of reference and an unending fund of inspiration. Publishers, in many respects, have succeeded the earlier patrons of art. They provide an enormous source of commissioned work. Although the paintings are usually conceived for a commercial purpose, this art is attracting increasing interest in its own right.

This book features the work of Tim White, a contemporary artist who is currently occupied almost exclusively in this sphere. The main theme of his work is the projection of a completely realistic image, the basis of which is fantasy.

1

FLOWERS
1969

Apart from a cobra and three birds there are over 250 faces hidden in the flowers.

2

EGGS
1970

INTRODUCTION

Tim has an optimistic view of the role of Science
Fiction and Fantasy, finding it unfortunate that a
form of such variety should be so prone to
generalisation. A vast range of literature is
contained within its framework and in terms of
quality it encompasses both extremes. Each can be
entertaining, but more importantly the genre
provides an immense facility for creative thought.
For children it indulges an inquiring mind and the
works aimed at the adult market continue to
provide a channel for the imagination, rich in ideas.

As a medium, the opportunities offered to artists
are unparalleled. There is far more freedom than
ever before, both in the choice of subject and the
materials now available for execution. In order to
respond to a commerical market, however, it is
unrealistic to expect total freedom. Compromises

3

MORDRED
1970

must sometimes be made, for example, to accommodate the demands of an art director. Tim feels that this can be advantageous rather than restrictive. It provides both discipline and motivation, and an openness to valid criticism which is important to personal development. An artist is often too close to his own work to view it objectively.

The most prominent aspect of Tim's work is an almost obsessive attention to detail, a fascination which stems from certain lavishly illustrated books of his childhood. He was continually rewarded when he found that closer scrutiny of an illustration revealed hidden and incidental details which a cursory glance would have overlooked. Combining detail with a largely figurative approach to interpretation, he aims to create a realistic image, a convincing landscape of the imagination.

The source of inspiration varies with each painting. It may be a chapter, a passage or just a few words. Occasionally a book may coincide perfectly with a particularly strong image Tim had been fostering and which he is then able to develop. If the narrative does not lend itself to vivid imagery, he may employ a more symbolic approach that represents the overall mood of the book. Tim has also experimented with various photographic

4
MOSQUITO
1970

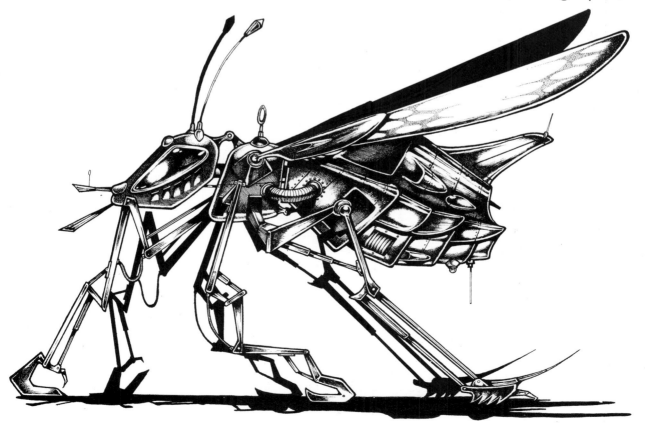

effects, a method which he had never seen applied to fantasy illustration. The out-of-focus result of blurring certain areas of a painting lends a more dimensional viewpoint and can draw attention to a particular image.

Ideas for each painting are developed through a rough stage. Tim might do several versions, experimenting first with variations of an image and then with colours. This method helps his imagination to focus even though the finished painting might evolve at a tangent. Although he experiments to varying degrees with other mediums, Tim prefers to work in gouache, finding it both effective and practical as oils often take weeks to dry properly.

Tim devotes a great deal of time to give plausibility to content. Taking life as a broad model, he develops ideas for both machinery and alien organisms in plasticine, studying lighting, function and manipulation. Organic creations especially, he feels, should respond to their environment. He finds, however, that there are definite barriers to acceptability, which correspond to our limited view of the universe. Similarly, much that at one time seemed to be the invention of a weird imagination is now accepted because communication has made the world a smaller, more accessible place. So it is necessary for alien conceptions to have a recognisable starting point because something that is wholly alien to us would find no frame of reference.

In producing book-cover artwork it is impossible to avoid presenting the reader with a personal interpretation of the contents. All work relies on individual response, however, and Tim hopes to offer an immediately recognisable image which will serve as a foundation for the observer's own imagination. This intention is vividly illustrated by the poems of Kenneth V. Bailey, on pages 31, 69 and 71. They were composed in response to several paintings which had been reproduced as postcards and they are included here by kind permission of the author. Commentaries to individual paintings have been included where it was felt that some form of explanation may be of interest. These are often in the form of a brief quotation from the relevant book.

TIM WHITE

Tim White was born in Kent in April 1952. His ambition to become an illustrator was formed very early in life and in 1968 he entered Medway College of Art to begin a course in general illustration. The following year, his first poster was published. In an atmosphere free from the restraints and pressures often imposed by commerical art, the college environment offered a unique opportunity to experiment and develop a personal style. Favouring pen and ink as a medium, much of the work he produced during this period was fantasy oriented.

In 1972 Tim left college and spent the first two years of his professional life as in illustrator in a number of advertising studios. The experience he gained proved valuable despite the limitations of the work, although he derived far more pleasure from an increasing number of freelance commissions in the area of Science Fiction and Fantasy. In 1974 he received his first book-cover commission for Arthur C. Clarke's *The Other Side of the Sky* (Corgi Books) and soon afterwards became a full-time freelance illustrator.

He has since produced well over a hundred book-cover paintings. Other work includes record sleeves, magazine illustrations, private commissions, film and other related projects. His work has also appeared in several exhibitions of Science Fiction and Fantasy art.

5

PURSUED
1972

6

METAL BUTTERFLY
1973

7
SHIP
1973

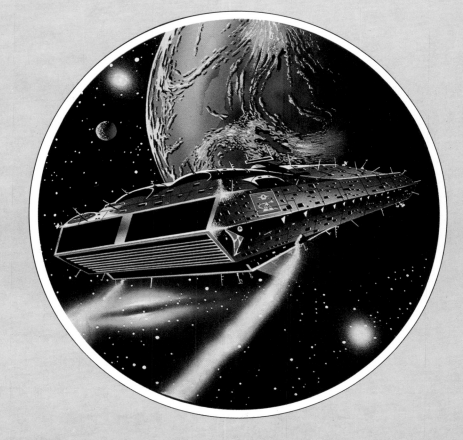

8
THE OTHER SIDE OF THE
SKY
1974

First cover commission.

9
MONUMENT
1974

10
THE LEGEND OF GX118
1974

11
WANDERING WORLDS
1975

12
STOPWATCH
1975

13

ICERIGGER
1975

Bruised and shaken, the occupants of a crashed escape shuttle venture out onto the frozen wastes of a cold and uncompromising world to confront a horde of potentially hostile inhabitants gliding over the ice towards them.

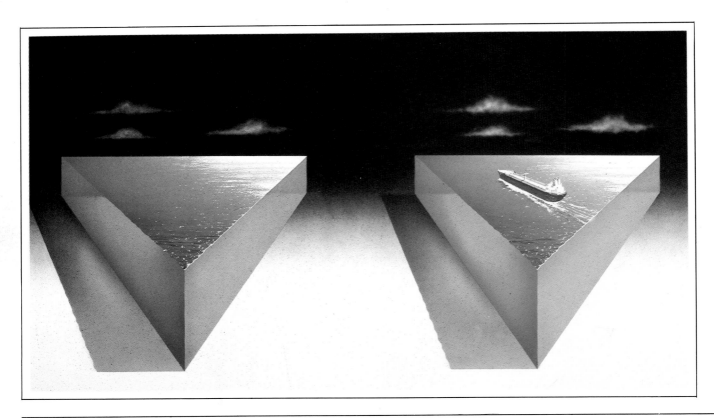

14

BERMUDA TRIANGLE
1975

15

THE FOG
1975

16
THE MAN WITH A
THOUSAND NAMES
1975

17
GREEN ODYSSEY
1975

19

HUMMING SHIP
1975

In some far system, where the moon-lit evening skies
Are splashed by lights of verging nebulae,
Men heard our sullen humming symphony –
Heard over swamp-filled forest-land the cries
Of frightened birds, and saw our bright and cutting beams
Piercing their planet's skin, probing its seams
Of mineral and rock. And to that lightning rod
They knelt and prayed, as to a sudden god.

Our asteroid, hard-warped by stress of interstellar flight
Into hypnotic multitudes of planes,
Moves demon-like on dazzling, disappearing vanes
Above these lowlands, splintering the tropic night
With emerald flares, disrupting cloaks of trees and moss
Long centuries have spread across the plain, fountaining dross
Of roots and soil and crystal spar to make their bore,
Lasers unmasking gulfs of fissionable ore.

The humming spells our power; and yet its plaintive undertone
Tells of our sadness at the universe's rim.
As gods we seem, omnipotent, inviolate, our hymn
Of power surrounding us; yet more a prison than a throne
Is our great mining ship to us. We travel far,
Free-faring gloriously from star to coloured star –
But home is distant, time is harsh, and we
Have more of exile in us than of deity.

© Kenneth V. Bailey, 1978

20
THE RAIN GODDESS
1975

21
GLORY ROAD (1)
1975

22
'SALEM'S LOT
1975

23

WAITING TO HEAR FROM
WILLIAM
1975

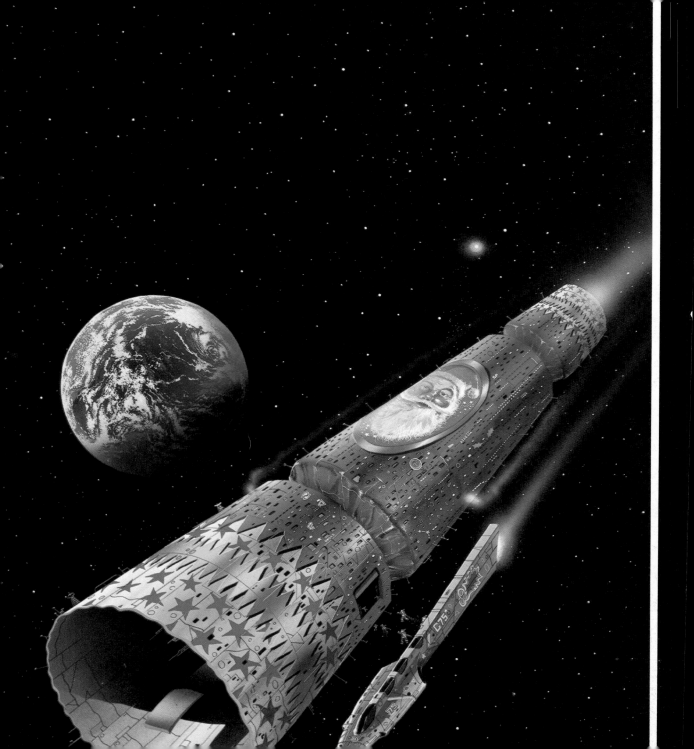

25

THE UNPLEASANT
PROFESSION OF JONATHAN
HOAG
1975

'. . . They were laughing at
him, goading him, trying to
get him to make a false move.
He knew it – they had been
plotting against him for days,
trying to shake his nerve.
They watched him out of
every mirror in the house,
ducking back when he tried to
catch them at it. The sons of
the Bird . . .'

26

OTHER WORLDS
1975

Written in about 1650 by
Cyrano de Bergerac, the
following quotation is taken
from a short story entitled
'The States and Empires of
the Sun' and depicts a quaint,
though surprisingly
far-sighted, conception of
space travel under solar
power.

'. . . It was a large, very light
box, which closed very
tightly. It was six feet high or
thereabouts and three feet
square. There was a hole in
the bottom of the box; on top
of the roof, which also had
one in it, I placed a vessel of
crystal, which was similarly
pierced. This was made in the
form of a very capacious
globe, with a neck which was
finished off evenly and fitted
into the aperture I had
fashioned in the top of the
box.

'This vessel was
deliberately constructed with
a number of surfaces,
however, in the form of an
icosahedron and, as each
facet was both convex and
concave, my ball produced
the effect of a dazzling
mirror . . .'

27
ENEMY WITHIN THE SKULL
1976

28
BRING THE JUBILEE
1975

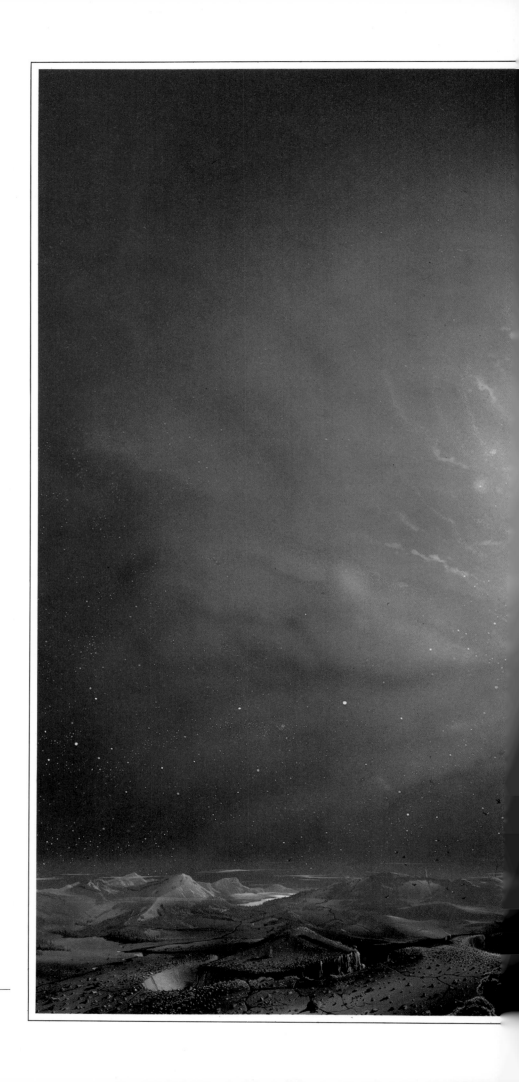

29
JEWEL OF JARHEN
1976

30
GUERNICA NIGHT
1976

31
BRAINWAVE
1976

32
BORDERLINE
1976

33
TRADING POST
1976

34
SEETEE ALERT
1976

35

EXPEDITION TO EARTH
1976

The painting illustrates an
Arthur C. Clarke short story
entitled 'Encounter in the
Dawn'. Mankind visits Earth a
thousand centuries before
Babylon.

36

A SCENT OF NEW-MOWN
HAY
1976

'. . . The most dreadful thing about it is this. In no instance does the victim die . . . This thing does not kill. It doesn't need to. It is against its interest to kill. It blends its cells with those of the victim, incorporates itself with it.

'In the final form you have a creature that retains a basic human structure and yet its material is purely fungoid. You have a thing that can see and move and very possibly retain some thought processes. Thoughts that if they do exist will have one aim and one alone. That of spreading itself to others. . .'

37
EARTH ENSLAVED
1976

38
EATER OF WORLDS
1976

39
NOT BEFORE TIME
1976

40
STRANGE INVADERS
1976

41
MOTHERSHIP IN SPACE
1976

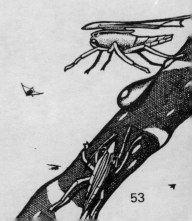

42
COSMIC SAXOPHONE
1976

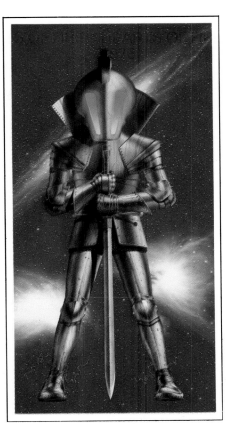

43
HEARTS OF FIRE
1976

44
MEMOIRS OF A
SPACEWOMAN
1976

45
LORD OF THE SPIDERS
1976

'. . . The city seemed to be one large building sprawling through the jungle. It appeared to grow out of the jungle, merge with it, be part of it. It was of dark, ancient obsidian and, in crevices, earth and seeds had fallen so that small trees and shrubs grew out of the city. There were ziggaurats and domes all appearing to flow together in the half-light. It was easy to believe that this was some strange freak of nature, that rock had simply flowed and solidified into the appearance of a city . . .'

THE PAST THROUGH
TOMORROW (Volumes 1 and
2)

47

CITY OF THE BEAST
1976

'. . . The strange oval ship
was even more beautiful at
close view. It was evidently
incredibly ancient. There was
the aura of millennia of
existence about it . . .'

48

DRAGON DRONE
1977

An artefact from a long-forgotten war. A terror weapon which continues relentlessly to seek its victims, scouring remote planets vast distances apart in search of its selected prey. A self-sustaining war machine.

49

DEATH CLOUD
1977

'. . . The whole landscape
changed from a sparkling,
lively scene to a dismal bleak
one. Everyone had the feeling
of death: that the hand of
death had come over the
land . . .'

50

THE RINGWAY VIRUS
1977

51
THE VISUAL ENCYCLOPEDIA
OF SCIENCE FICTION
1977

52
CROC
1977

53

THOSE WHO WATCH
1977

We watched when earth was but a wisp of gas.
We watch it now,
Seeing the slow clouds pass across it face
Tracing those lucent spider-threads which show
The paths from maze to maze of clustered life,
Fragile as patterns on a spread of lace.

We map the wilderness: the spines of ice
And snow, the polar seas and empty spans
Of sand and desert scrub. We know
The glow of burning cities and the plumes
Of war. We are not foe; we are not friend.
We send our knowledge to the furthest ends of space.
We will not go away – through birth to death
Of species and of race we are the watchers of the earth.
Our mission is to monitor each spasm
Of its history, each breath it breathes,
To catch and give to all the galaxy
True visions of our ever-rolling base.

© Kenneth V. Bailey, 1978

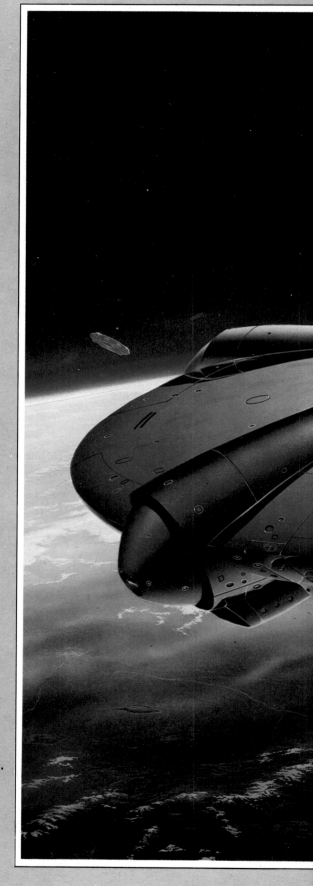

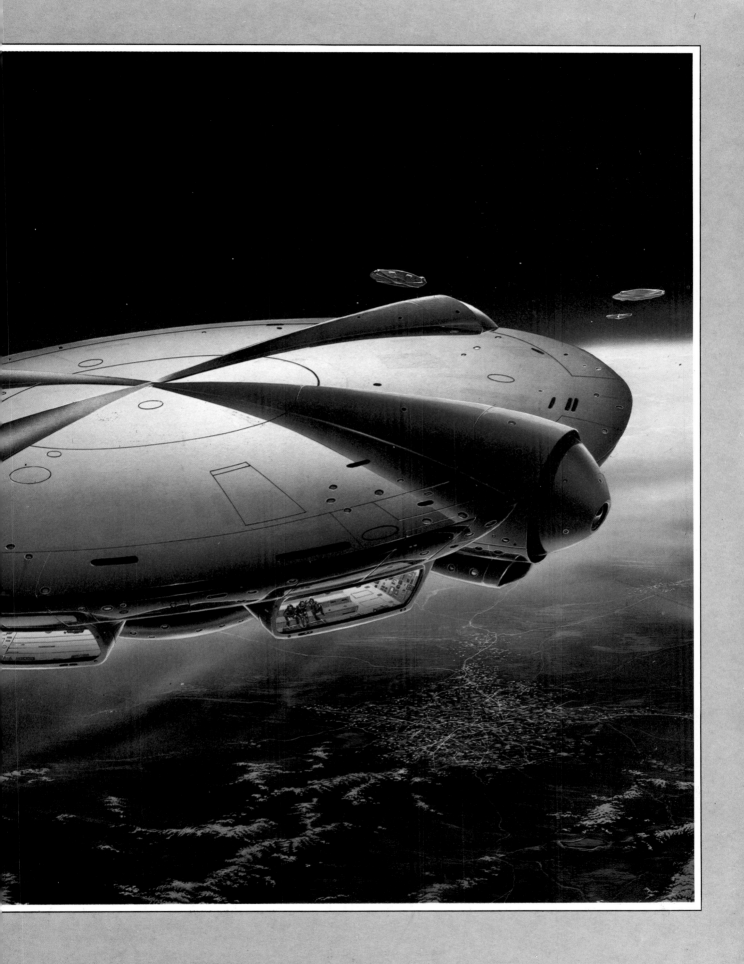

54

RING AROUND THE SUN
1977

'. . . No mouse, but something else – something that scuttled in the night, knowing that he would think it was a mouse; a thing that had scared the cat which knew it was no mouse, and a thing that would not be attracted to traps.

'An electronic spy, he speculated, a scuttling, scurrying, listening thing that watched his every moment, a thing that stored what it heard and saw for future reference or transmitted directly the knowledge that it gained. But direct to whom? And why? . . .

55
THROUGH A GLASS
CLEARLY
1977

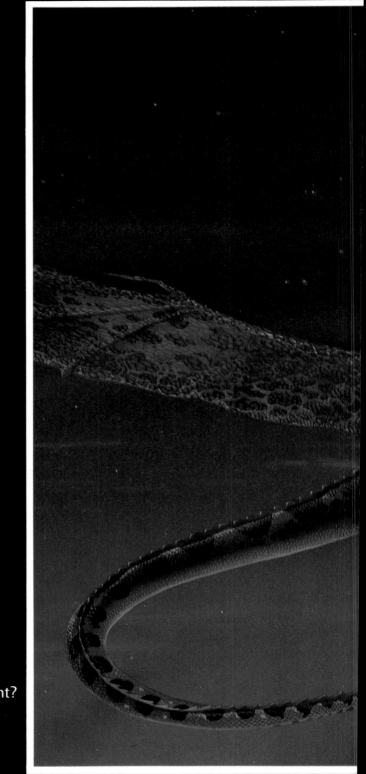

56

EVENING FLIGHT
1977

In the long planetary twilight
Dragons drift by,
Transparent wings star-studded as the night
Through which they fly,
Their hazy breath is mingled with the ash
Of stars long dead,
Their dance is coiled about a sun's last flash,
Stormy and red.

Are they the issue of a planet's seas,
Conquering air,
Great saurians that leave the cliffs and trees,
Their earth-bound lair,
To swing above the clouds in silent chase
Of soaring prey
Which dives and loops about the edge of space
Twixt night and day?

Or is this flying snake a demi urge,
The aeon of old,
A universe enfolded in its wings – the surge
Of galaxies untold
Expanding with their beat, each nova burst
Shining as scales
Flaked from its lashing tail and wide-dispersed
On cosmic gales?

Or is leviathan a finite beast,
A chain of births –
And yet a universe, its span increased
As moons and earths
And suns and galaxies grow with its evening flight?
Are systems bound
In microscopic wings which fill each night
With insect sound?

© Kenneth V. Bailey, 1978

58

ASSIGNMENT IN ETERNITY (1)
1977

High in the rugged lunar landscape and set in a steep crater wall, a retractable dome provides a terrestrial environment for the occupants of a large private estate. Solar energy, absorbed by instruments set in exposed areas about the crater, supplies all power to the structure.

59
THE RAINBOW DEATHS
1977

60
THE MOON IS A HARSH
MISTRESS
1977

61
THE COLD CASH WAR
1977

62

REVOLT IN 2100
1977

63

DARK SIDE OF THE SUN
1977

Taken directly from an earlier
black and white line drawing
(page. 9) which coincided
with the plot of the book:
micro-engineering produces
an unobtrusive surveillance
device.

64

ALIEN CITY
1977

Another view of the same alien city illustrated in LORD OF THE SPIDERS. This time from the north-west, in the mountains high above the forest.

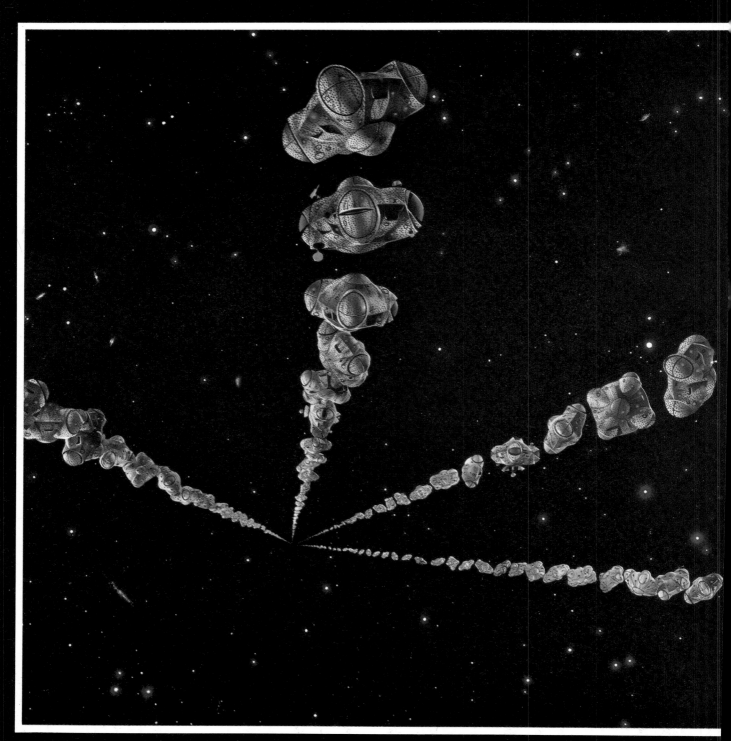

65

SILENT PROCESSION OF
SPACE TUMBLERS
1977

66

THE DAY AFTER
TOMORROW
1977

Sometimes a simple image
gives a more dramatic effect.
A deliberate effort was
necessary to refrain from
adding more detail.

67
GLORY ROAD (2)
1977

68

AMERGIN AND GORVENAL
1977

Amergin points to the crater
from which the mysterious
ball of light climbed into the
heavens. Whatever it was
kept the crater green, holding
back the encroaching snow
and turning the surrounding
ground into a steamy swamp.

ROGUE GOLEM
1978

71

SPACE CITY COMPLEX
1978

Spinning from a common centre for gravity, the outer edge of a vast and ancient space colony reflects the blue glow of a nearby planet. Functioning as an independent society, it is a prosperous trading centre and a colossal population dwells within the mycelium-like network. An enormous variety of solar domes are scattered about its surface. Many support the cultivation areas which provide the colony's food and raw materials, others are parks and residential zones, while more specialist domes can create complete alien environments. The structure is in the continual process of expansion and repair.

72
ASSIGNMENT IN ETERNITY (2)
1978

73
STRANGER IN A STRANGE
LAND
1978

74
THOUGHTWORLD
1978

75
SUPERMIND
1978

76
EQUATOR
1978

77
THE INTERPRETER
1978

Hunted and in fear of their lives, the stranded members of an exploration team anxiously await rescue.

Above them their mother ship struggles to touch down, her engines illuminating the surrounding landscape.

THE TAR-AIYM KRANG
1978

80
ORPHAN STAR
1978

81
A TOUCH OF STRANGE
1978

82

THE END OF THE MATTER
1978

Closely watched from the
surrounding vegetation, an
empty aircar hovers gently on
a gravity cushion awaiting
the return of its occupants.

83
THE LION GAME
1978

84
THE MAN WHO SOLD THE
MOON
1978

85

THE SANTAROGA BARRIER
1978

A monstrous sixteen-wheeled multi-purpose buggy. The machine has extendable legs and drive to all four sets of wheels, all steerable, making it an effective vehicle over most kinds of terrain. The legs and independent suspension absorb most shocks in motion while the cab remains relatively stable. It is able to carry quite large loads under the belly and has a wide range of applications, both civilian and military.

86
VIMANA
1978

89
GATHER DARKNESS
1978

90
UNDER A CALCULATING
STAR
1978

91

TWENTY HOUSES OF THE ZODIAC
1979

From a short story entitled 'High Tide' By Elisabeth Vonarburg.

'. . . Communication by way of colours? With whom? Exchanges within swarms are not operated visually, olfits use ultra-sounds. Anyway, inside the swarm there is no need for it: the whole swarm is the "olfit", a collective form of being . . .

'It's such a weird light when all the moons are on parade, yellow, blue, pink with multiple shadows . . . All of a sudden, one shadow moves faster than the others, shifting colours whimsically transmute by the light of the moons, a swarm of olfits whirls past the window into the room. What do they want? The tenuous chirping becomes more insistent, the swarm eddies around the furniture, the patterns giddily merge into each other. It must be urgent. It's important . . .'

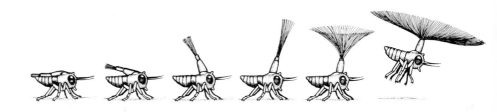

92
BLOODHYPE
1979

93
THE LIGHT FANTASTIC
1979

Volume One in a collection of
short stories by Alfred Bester.

94
STAR LIGHT, STAR BRIGHT
1979

In this second volume of
short stories, Alfred Bester
explores one of science
fiction's most recurrent
themes – the threat of high
technology out of control. In
the illustrated story a rogue
satellite becomes god over its
creators – to rule Earth for
twenty years before its orbit
finally decays.

95

STRATA
1979

After the storm has passed the less specialised insects of a wet, fungoid world enjoy a brief respite for hunting and gathering food before the next violent storm is upon them.

96
PROJECT BARRIER
1979

In the tracks of its superior, a small robot analyser collects samples of the sparse flora in the thin atmosphere of a desolate asteroid. Even the most diminutive member of the team has fallen victim to an unprecedented outbreak of megalomania and broods secretly on a Machiavellian plot to improve its position in a larger robot hierachy.

INVOLUTION OCEAN
1979

In an ocean of fine dust these strange crab-like creatures are well adapted to their environment. Spending most of their time submerged, they can also move quite rapidly across the surface with the aid of their saucer-shaped feet and they are acutely aware of any vibration in the dust. Highly polished shells repel the adhering dust and its abrasive qualities, and, when submerging, antennae retract and transparent shutters close over their eyes for protection.

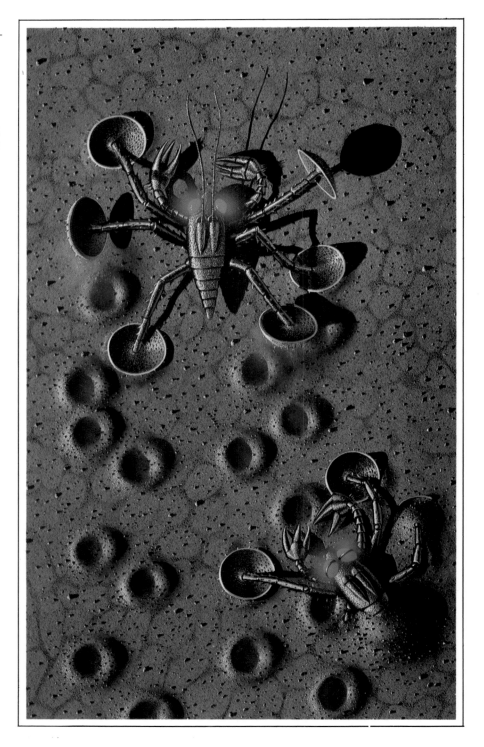

98
DYING INSIDE
1979

99
MISSION TO MOULOKIN
1979

100
THE CITY OF THE SUN
1979

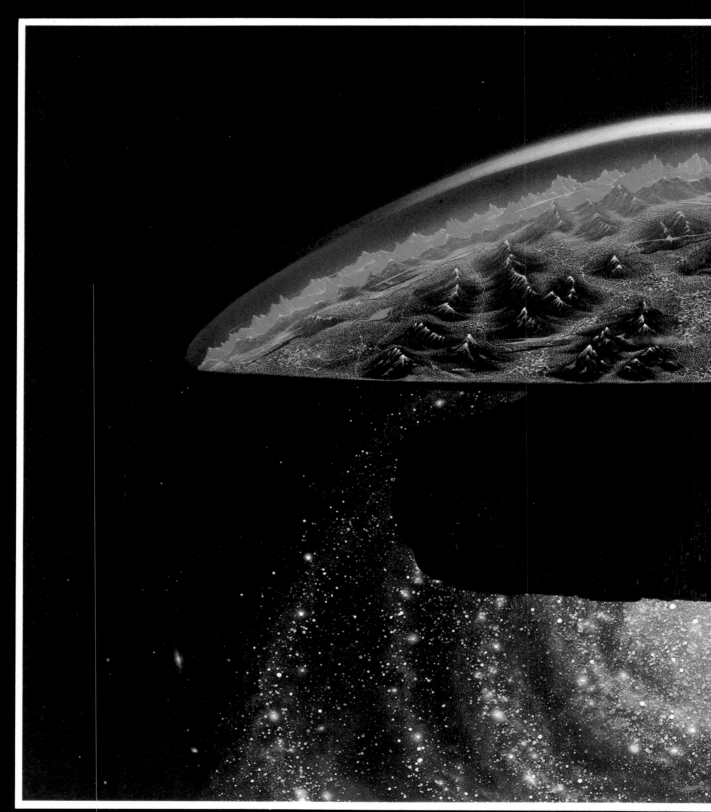

101

MACROLIFE
1979

The collective sciences of
different races within our
galaxy combine in wondrous
control over the elements to
finally escape the confines of
this galaxy to search the void
of intergalactic space.

THE JESUS INCIDENT
1979

104
THE FIRES OF LAN-KERN
1979

After the nuclear holocaust
the veneer of civilisation will
vanish and a dark age ensue,
where might prevails and the
meek suffer. Superstition will

gain ascendance over
rationality. With technology
destroyed and the principles
forgotten our reality would
soon recede into legend.

106
THE NUMBER OF THE BEAST
1979

107

Plasticine model
Height: 230mm. Acrylic
paints

'. . . When he was within five
metres of them, one turned
and pointed a pencil-like
instrument at him. Masse
was stopped in his tracks,
unable to move . . .
According to Masse's
testimony the creatures were
less than four feet tall, and
were clad in close-fitting
gray-green clothes, but
without head covering. They
had pumpkinlike heads, high
fleshy cheeks, large eyes
which slanted away, mouths
without lips and very pointed
chins . . .'
   A report of the occupants
of an UFO, sighted in a
lavender field near Valensole,
France, from *Flying Saucer
Review.*

108
OUT OF MY MIND
1979

109
UFO UK
1980

110
THE SPACE MACHINE
1980

111
PERILOUS PLANETS
1980

Seemingly with little hope, a group of quogs cling desperately to the tallest tree on their submerged island. The hardy Mee Haw tree offers a precarious refuge. Anxious eyes scan the heavens for a break in the storm. The angry and unpredictable wine-coloured sea rises in freak floods once in several generations, threatening their very survival.

113
RAINBOW DESERT
1980

114
THE HEAVEN MAKERS
1980

115

116
TOO MANY MAGICIANS
1980

TECHNICAL AND PUBLISHING DETAILS

1 Unpublished
Size: 290mm x 210mm

2 Unpublished
Size: 130mm x 155mm

3 Unpublished
Size: 190mm x 213mm

4 Unpublished
Size: 200mm x 215mm

5 Unpublished
Size: 155mm x 190mm

6 Unpublished
Size: 310mm x 221mm

7 Unpublished
Size: 265 x 303mm

8 Cover painting for THE OTHER SIDE OF THE SKY, by Arthur C. Clarke. Published by Corgi Books (1974).
Size: 125mm diameter

9 Cover painting for MONUMENT, by Lloyd Biggle Jr. Published by New English Library (1975).
Size: 269mm x 365mm

10 Content illustration for short story THE LEGEND OF GX118. *Science Fiction Monthly* magazine. Published by New English Library (1974). Published as a poster by New English Library (1975).
Size: 408mm x 288mm

11 Content illustration for short story GREEN IN THE EVENING. *Science Fiction Monthly* magazine. Published by New English Library (1975). Subsequently reproduced as cover painting for WANDERING WORLDS, by Terry Greenhough.
Size: 408mm x 283mm

12 Cover painting for STOPWATCH, edited by George Hay. Published by New English Library (1975).
Size: 271mm x 327mm

13 Cover painting for ICERIGGER, by Alan Dean Foster. Published by New English Library (1975).
Size: 274mm x 607mm

14 Cover painting for THE BERMUDA TRIANGLE, by Lawrence David Kusche. Published by New English Library (1975).
Size: 343mm x 486mm

15 Cover painting for THE FOG, by James Herbert. Published by New English Library (1975).
Size: 285mm x 653mm

16 Cover painting for THE MAN WITH A THOUSAND NAMES, by A. E. Van Vogt. Published by Sidgwick & Jackson (1975).
Size: 253mm x 325mm

17 Cover painting commissioned by Sphere Books. Unpublished.
Size: 251mm x 330mm

18 Cover painting for THE DARKNESS ON DIAMONDIA, by A. E. Van Vogt. Published by Sidgwick & Jackson (1975).
Size: 250mm x 329mm

19 Cover painting for GALAXY OF THE LOST, by Gregory Kern. Published by Mews Books (1976). Subsequently published as a card titled HUMMING SHIP.
Size: 300mm x 386mm

20 Cover painting for THE RAIN GODDESS, by Peter Stiff. Published by New English Library (1976).

21 Cover painting for GLORY ROAD, by Robert A. Heinlein. Published by New English Library (1976), hardcover edition.
Size: 305mm x 691mm

22 Cover painting for 'SALEM'S LOT, by Stephen King. Published by New English Library.
Size: 302mm x 521mm

23 Unpublished.
Size: 237mm x 404mm

24 Cover painting for SCIENCE FICTION MONTHLY magazine, Christmas edition 1975. Published by New English Library.
Size: 400mm x 278mm

25 Cover painting for THE UNPLEASANT PROFESSION OF JONATHAN HOAG, by Robert A. Heinlein. Published by New English Library (1976).
Size: 362mm x 210mm

26 Cover painting for OTHER WORLDS, by Cyrano de Bergerac. Published by New English Library (1976).
Size: 330mm x 388mm

27 Cover painting for ENEMY WITHIN THE SKULL, by Gregory Kern. Published by Mews Books (1976).
Size: 292mm x 451mm

28 Cover painting for BRING THE JUBILEE, by Ward Moore. Published by New English Library (1976).
Size: 302mm x 693mm

29 Cover painting for JEWEL OF JARHEN, by Gregory Kern. Published by Mews Books (1976).
Size: 328mm x 398mm

30 Cover painting for GUERNICA NIGHT, by Barry N. Malzberg. Published by New English Library (1977).
Size: 310mm x 704mm

31 Cover painting for BRAIN WAVE, by Poul Anderson. Published by New English Library (1976). Subsequently published as a card.
Size: 338mm x 345mm

32 Cover painting for BORDERLINE, by Vercors. Published by New English Library (1976).
Size: 358mm x 222mm

33 Content illustration for short story entitled TRADING POST. *S.F. Digest* Magazine, New English Library (1976).
Size: 382mm x 560mm

34 Cover painting for SEETEE ALERT, by Gregory Kern. Published by Mews Books (1976).
Size: 378mm x 457mm

35 Cover painting for EXPEDITION TO EARTH, by Arthur C. Clarke. Published by New English Library (1976).
Size: 370mm x 476mm

36 Cover painting for A SCENT OF NEW-MOWN HAY, by John Blackburn. Published by New English Library (1976).
Size: 396mm x 241mm

37 Cover painting for BETWEEN PLANETS, by Robert A. Heinlein. Published by New English Library (1977). Subsequently published as a card titled EARTH ENSLAVED.
Size: 340mm x 445mm

38 Cover painting for THE EATER OF WORLDS, by Gregory Kern. Published by Mews Books (1976).
Size: 339mm x 420mm

39 Cover painting for NOT BEFORE TIME, by John Brunner. Published by New English Library (1979).
Size: 344mm x 442mm

40 Cover painting for THE STRANGE INVADERS, by Alun Llewellyn. Published by New English Library (1977).
Size: 340mm x 435mm

41 Unpublished.
Size: 685mm x 343mm

42 Private commission COSMIC SAXOPHONE. Collection: Stephen Pearson.
Size: 697mm x 349mm

43 Album cover painting for HEARTS OF FIRE, Stray. Pye Records (1976).
Size: 680mm x 340mm

44 Cover painting for MEMOIRS OF A SPACEWOMAN, by Naomi Mitchison. Published by New English Library (1977).
Size: 324mm x 407mm

45 Cover painting for LORD OF THE SPIDERS, by Michael Moorcock. Published by New English Library (1979).
Size: 343mm x 409mm

46 Cover painting for THE PAST THROUGH TOMORROW (Volumes 1 and 2), by Robert A. Heinlein. Published by New English Library (1977).
Size: 369mm x 717mm

47 Cover painting for CITY OF THE BEAST, by Michael Moorcock. Published by New English Library (1977).
Size: 369mm x 476mm

48 Painting for DRAGON 1979 calendar. Published by Dragon's World Ltd.
Size: 368mm x 508mm

49 Cover painting for DEATH CLOUD, by Michael Mannion. Published by New English Library (1977).
Size: 330mm x 427mm

50 Cover painting for THE RINGWAY VIRUS, by Russell Foreman. Published by New English Library (1977).
Size: 280mm x 387mm

51 Cover painting for THE VISUAL ENCYCLOPEDIA OF SCIENCE FICTION. Published by Pan Books (1977).
Size: 312mm x 650mm

52 Cover painting for CROC, by David James. Published by New English Library (1977).
Size: 396mm x 241mm

53 Cover painting for THOSE WHO WATCH, by Robert Silverberg. Published by New English Library (1977). Subsequently published as a card.
Size: 343mm x 442mm

54 Cover painting for RING AROUND THE SUN, by Clifford D. Simak. Published by New English Library (1979).
Size: 415mm x 274mm

55 Cover painting for THROUGH A GLASS CLEARLY, by Isaac Asimov. Published by New English Library (1977).
Size: 468mm x 315mm

56 Painting for DRAGON 1979 calendar. Published by Dragon's World Ltd. Published as a card.
Size: 345mm x 476mm

57 Painting for DRAGON 1979 calendar. Published by Dragon's World Ltd. Published as a card.
Size: 318mm x 437mm

58 Cover painting for ASSIGNMENT IN ETERNITY (1), by Robert A. Heinlein. Published by New English Library (1977).
Size: 387mm x 245mm

59 Cover painting for THE RAINBOW DEATHS, by John Churchward. Published by New English Library (1977).
Size: 418mm x 258mm

60 Cover painting for THE MOON IS A HARSH MISTRESS, by Robert A. Heinlein. Published by New English Library (1977).
Size: 357mm x 227mm

61 Cover painting for THE COLD CASH WAR, by Robert Asprin. Published by New English Library (1977).
Size: 455mm x 301mm

62 Cover painting for REVOLT IN 2100, by Robert A. Heinlein. Published by New English Library (1977).
Size: 375mm x 231mm

63 Cover painting for THE DARK SIDE OF THE SUN, by Terry Pratchett. Published by New English Library (1978).
Size: 388mm x 237mm

64 Private commission: ALIEN CITY
Size: 454mm x 500mm

65 From the Dragon's World/Paper Tiger Book LIVING IN SPACE. Edited by Roger Dean.
Size: 356mm x 705mm

66 Cover painting for THE DAY AFTER TOMORROW, by Robert A. Heinlein. Published by New English Library (1978).
Size: 402mm x 237mm

67 Cover painting for GLORY ROAD, by Robert A. Heinlein. Published by New English Library (1978), paperback.
Size: 387mm x 246mm

68 AMERGIN AND GORVENAL. Painting commissioned by Ridley Scott. For development of a film based on Tristan and Iseult, for Paramount Pictures.
Size: 349mm x 697mm

69 Cover painting for THORNS, by Robert Silverberg. Published by New English Library (1978).
Size: 387mm x 237mm

70 Cover painting for ROGUE GOLEM, by Ernest M. Kenyon. Published by New English Library (1979).
Size: 445mm x 265mm

71 From the Dragon's World/Paper Tiger Book LIVING IN SPACE. Edited by Roger Dean.
Size: 349mm x 699mm

72 Cover painting for ASSIGNMENT IN ETERNITY (2), by Robert A. Heinlein. Published by New English Library (1978).
Size: 387mm x 235mm

73 Cover painting for STRANGER IN A STRANGE LAND, by Robert A. Heinlein. Published by New English Library (1978).
Size: 387mm x 235mm

74 Cover painting for THOUGHTWORLD, by Terry Greenhough. Published by New English Library (1978).
Size: 447mm x 265mm

75 Cover painting for SUPERMIND, by A. E. Van Vogt. Published by New English Library (1979).
Size: 436mm x 271mm

76 Cover painting for EQUATOR, by Brian Aldiss. Published by New English Library.
Size: 357mm x 227mm

77 Cover painting for THE INTERPRETER, by Brian Aldiss. Published by New English Library.
Size: 367mm x 218mm

78 Cover painting for THE WITLING, by Vernor Vinge. Published by Hamlyn (1978).
Size: 387mm x 236mm

79 Cover painting for THE TAR-AIYM KRANG, by Alan Dean Foster. Published by New English Library (1979).
Size: 417mm x 250mm

80 Cover painting for ORPHAN STAR, by Alan Dean Foster. Published by New English Library (1979).
Size: 430mm x 283mm

81 Cover painting for A TOUCH OF STRANGE, by Theodore Sturgeon. Published by Hamlyn (1979).
Size: 388mm x 236mm

82 Cover painting for THE END OF THE MATTER, by Alan Dean Foster. Published by New English Library (1979).
Size: 387mm x 237mm

83 Cover painting for THE LION GAME, by James H. Schmit. Published by Hamlyn (1979).
Size: 387mm x 237mm

84 Cover painting for THE MAN WHO SOLD THE MOON, by Robert A. Heinlein. Published by New English Library (1979).
Size: 387mm x 236mm

85 Cover painting for THE SANTAROGA BARRIER, by Frank Herbert. Published by New English Library (1979).
Size: 445mm x 265mm

86 Unpublished.
Size: 408mm x 597mm

87 Cover painting for CRITICAL THRESHOLD, by Brian M. Stableford. Published by Hamlyn (1979).
Size: 387mm x 234mm

88 Cover painting for WILDEBLOOD'S EMPIRE, by Brian M. Stableford. Published by Hamlyn.
Size: 417mm x 250mm

89 Cover painting for GATHER DARKNESS, by Fritz Leiber. Published by New English Library (1979).
Size: 418mm x 251mm

90 Cover painting for UNDER A CALCULATING STAR, by John Morressy. Published by New English Library (1979).
Size: 388mm x 237mm

91 Cover painting for TWENTY HOUSES OF THE ZODIAC, edited by Maxim Jakubowski. Published by New English Library (1979).
Size: 418mm x 251mm

92 Cover painting for BLOODHYPE, by Alan Dean Foster. Published by New English Library (1979).
Size: 445mm x 265mm

93 Cover painting for THE LIGHT FANTASTIC, by Alfred Bester. Published by Fontana (1979).
Size: 418mm x 250mm

94 Cover painting for STAR LIGHT, STAR BRIGHT, by Alfred Bester. Published by Fontana (1979).
Size: 418mm x 250mm

95 Cover painting for STRATA, by Terry Pratchett. Commission: Colin Smythe Limited, Publishers.
Size: 413mm x 244mm

96 Cover painting for PROJECT BARRIER, by Daniel F. Galouye. Published by Hamlyn, (1979).
Size: 417mm x 250mm

97 Cover painting for INVOLUTION OCEAN, by Bruce Sterling. Published by New English Library (1979).
Size: 413mm x 245mm

98 Cover painting for DYING INSIDE, by Robert Silverberg. Published by New English Library (1979).
Size: 418mm x 252mm

99 Cover painting for MISSION TO MOULOKIN, by Alan Dean Foster. Published by New English Library (1979).
Size: 423 x 279mm

100 Cover painting for THE CITY OF THE SUN, by Brian M. Stableford. Published by Hamlyn (1979).
Size: 445mm x 265mm

101 Cover painting for MACROLIFE, by George Zebrowski. Published by Futura Publications (1980).
Size: 382mm x 485mm

102 Unpublished.
Size: 445mm x 248mm

103 Cover painting for THE JESUS INCIDENT, by Frank Herbert and Bill Ransom. Published by Futura Publications (1980).
Size: 417mm x 250mm

104 Cover painting for THE FIRES OF LAN-KERN, by Peter Tremayne. Published by Magnum (1980).
Size: 385mm x 236mm

105 Back cover painting for THE JESUS INCIDENT, by Frank Herbert and Bill Ransom. Published by Futura Publications (1980).
Size: 416mm x 297mm

106 Cover painting for THE NUMBER OF THE BEAST, by Robert A. Heinlein. Published by New English Library (1980).
Size: 441mm x 285mm

107 Plasticine model.

108 Cover painting for OUT OF MY MIND, by John Brunner. Published by New English Library (1980).
Size: 401mm x 248mm

109 Cover painting for UFO UK, by Peter Paget. Published by New English Library (1980).
Size: 418mm x 250mm

110 Cover painting for THE SPACE MACHINE, by Christopher Priest. Published by Futura Publications (1980).
Size: 378mm x 489mm

111 Cover painting for PERILOUS PLANETS, edited by Brian Aldiss. Published by Futura Publications (1980).
Size: 375mm x 486mm

112 Cover painting for THE OUTCASTS OF HEAVEN BELT by Joan D'Vinge. Published by Futura Publication (1980).
Size: 371mm x 464mm

113 Unpublished.
Size: 215mm x 300mm

114 Cover painting for THE HEAVEN MAKERS, by Frank Herbert. Published by New English Library (1980).
Size: 418mm x 250mm

115 Unpublished.
Size: 367mm x 248mm
Photograph: Matt White

116 Cover painting for TOO MANY MAGICIANS, by Randall Garrett. Published by Futura Publications (1980).
Size: 377mm x 483mm

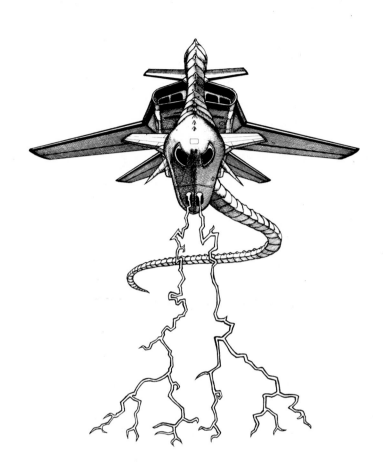